THE OTHER 637 BEST THINGS ANYBODY EVER SAID

"I have read your book and much like it."
Moses Hadas

"If you can't annoy somebody, there is little point in writing."
Kingsley Amis

"The covers of this book are too far apart."
Ambrose Bierce

"A person who publishes a book appears willfully in public with his pants down."
Edna St. Vincent Millay

"Good swiping is an art in itself."
Jules Feiffer

THE OTHER 637

BEST THINGS ANYBODY EVER SAID

Chosen and arranged by

Robert Byrne

FAWCETT CREST • NEW YORK

A Fawcett Crest Book
Published by Ballantine Books
Copyright © 1984 by Robert Byrne

Library of Congress Catalog Card Number: 84-45057

ISBN 0-449-20762-5

This edition published by arrangement with Atheneum

Manufactured in the United States of America

First Ballantine Books Edition: November 1985

To
Tom Stewart,
who has kept so much egg off my face

CONTENTS

⊷◉н◉↝

Introduction

PART ONE

Theology, Self-love, Self-abuse, Love, Sex, Wedlock, Kids, Drink, Death, Comedy, Men and Women, War, Money, Work, and a great deal more

PART TWO

Advice, Health, Food, Life Itself, America, Psychoses, Books, Writers, Music, Show Business, Animals, Doctors, Presidents, Politics, Sports, and much else

PART THREE

Miscellaneous

INTRODUCTION

My first collection of mostly humorous quotations was published in 1982 and was titled *The 637 Best Things Anybody Ever Said*, which might make you think that the sequel deals with the second best. Not true. These—the quotes in the book you are now holding—are in fact the 637 best things anybody ever said. In titling the first collection, I lied.

Most books of this sort are too full of chaff. For every quote you can use in conversation witout being thrown down the stairs as an intolerable bore there are pages of the pompous, the banal, and the so what? The aim here is to present nothing but kernels of wheat. Open the book anywhere; if you don't find a gem that makes you smile at least inwardly, you should ask your doctor if you are clinically dead.

Quotes are generally grouped by subject. Subjects follow each other sometimes at random and sometimes in a way to encourage reading pages consecutively, never according to the alphabet. In Part One, it struck me as logical to arrange Love, Sex, Wedlock, Kids, Drink, Death, and Comedy in that order.

It has often been noted by researchers into pith that the wages of the world are funniest when they are cynical rather than sentimental. That, and not any presumed sourness on my part, explains the preponderance of negative remarks. The number of anti-marriage quotes, for example, doesn't necessarily mean that I personally am against it. In truth, I like marriage, though I happen to be free of it at the moment.

Many thanks to the readers of *The 637 Best Things Anybody Ever Said*, which last I heard was still in print in both hardcover and paperback, who sent me their favorite lines. Their specific contributions are acknowledged in the Sources, References, and Notes.

A word about ascriptions. "Unknown" is used when I have been unable to discover the source. Readers may be better informed. "Anonymous" is used when I am convinced that the source not only is unknown but is going to stay unknown.

Birth and death dates are given only for historical figures.

The significance of the number 637 and other odds and ends are discussed in the Introduction to the earlier volume.

Robert Byrne
% Fawcett Books
201 East Fiftieth Street
New York, New York 10022

PART ONE

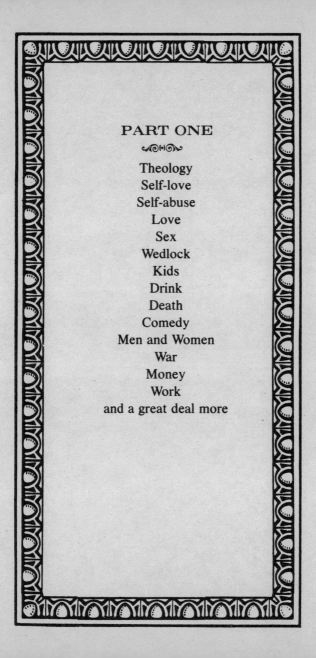

Theology
Self-love
Self-abuse
Love
Sex
Wedlock
Kids
Drink
Death
Comedy
Men and Women
War
Money
Work
and a great deal more

1

My theology, briefly, is that the universe was dictated but not signed. *Christopher Morley (1890–1957)*

2

God made everything out of nothing, but the nothingness shows through. *Paul Valéry (1871–1945)*

3

God was satisfied with his own work, and that is fatal.
Samuel Butler (1835–1902)

4

God is not dead but alive and well and working on a much less ambitious project. *Graffito*

5

Why attack God? He may be as miserable as we are.
Erik Satie (1866–1925)

Every day people are straying away from the church and going back to God.   *Lenny Bruce (1923–1966)*

Religion is what keeps the poor from murdering the rich.   *Napoleon (1769–1821)*

What if there had been room at the inn?
*Linda Festa on the
origins of Christianity*

Christ died for our sins. Dare we make his martyrdom meaningless by not committing them?   *Jules Feiffer*

Catholicism has changed tremendously in recent years. Now when Communion is served there is also a salad bar.   *Bill Marr*

11

Faith is believing what you know ain't so.

"A schoolboy" quoted by
Mark Twain (1835–1910)

12

Faith is under the left nipple.

Martin Luther (1483–1546)

13

Because I'm Jewish, a lot of people ask why I killed Christ. What can I say? It was an accident. It was one of those parties that got out of hand. I killed him because he wouldn't become a doctor.

Lenny Bruce (1923–1966)

14

Your chances of getting hit by lightning go up if you stand under a tree, shake your fist at the sky, and say, "Storms suck!" *Johnny Carson*

15

Trust in Allah, but tie your camel. *Arabian proverb*

☙◉❦◈❧

The last time I saw him he was walking down Lover's Lane holding his own hand.   *Fred Allen (1894–1956)*

17

The nice thing about egotists is that they don't talk about other people.   *Lucille S. Harper*

18

It is far more impressive when others discover your good qualities without your help.

Miss Manners (Judith Martin)

19

In an age when the fashion is to be in love with yourself, confessing to be in love with somebody else is an admission of unfaithfulness to one's beloved.

Russell Baker

20

If only it was as easy to banish hunger by rubbing the belly as it is to masturbate.

Diogenes the Cynic (412? to 323 B.C.)

21

Self-abuse is the most certain road to the grave.

Dr. George M. Calhoun in 1855

22

Many mothers are wholly ignorant of the almost universal prevalence of secret vice, or self-abuse, among the young. Why hesitate to say firmly and without quibble that personal abuse lies at the root of much of the feebleness, paleness, nervousness, and good-for-nothingness of the entire community?

Dr. J. H. Kellogg (1852–1943)

23

Masturbation! The amazing availability of it!

James Joyce (1882–1941)

24

Philosophy is to the real world as masturbation is to sex.   *Karl Marx (1818–1883)*

25

I was the best I ever had.   *Woody Allen*

26

The good thing about masturbation is that you don't have to dress up for it.   *Truman Capote*

27

My brain is my second favorite organ.   *Woody Allen*

✧◉H◉✧

28

Love is not the dying moan of a distant violin—it's the triumphant twang of a bedspring.
S. J. Perelman (1904–1979)

29

Love is what you've been through with somebody.
James Thurber (1894–1961)

30

Love is the delusion that one woman differs from another.   *H. L. Mencken (1880–1956)*

31

Love is being stupid together.

Paul Valéry (1871–1945)

32

Love is an obsessive delusion that is cured by marriage.
Dr. Karl Bowman (1888–1973)

33

Love is the only game that is not called on account of darkness.   *M. Hirschfield*

34

The greatest love is a mother's, then a dog's, then a sweetheart's.   *Polish proverb*

If I love you, what business is it of yours?
Johann von Goethe (1749–1832)

A man in love mistakes a pimple for a dimple.
Japanese proverb

A lover without indiscretion is no lover at all.
Thomas Hardy (1840–1928)

The most important thing in a relationship between a man and a woman is that one of them be good at taking orders. *Linda Festa*

In a great romance, each person basically plays a part that the other really likes. *Elizabeth Ashley*

I love Mickey Mouse more than any woman I've ever known.   *Walt Disney (1901–1966)*

I like young girls. Their stories are shorter.
Tom McGuane

The most romantic thing any woman ever said to me in bed was "Are you sure you're not a cop?"
Larry Brown

Someday we'll look back on this moment and plow into a parked car.   *Evan Davis*

Sex is dirty only when it's done right.   *Woody Allen*

For flavor, instant sex will never supersede the stuff you have to peel and cook.   *Quentin Crisp*

46

Why won't you let me kiss you goodnight? Is it something I said?   *Tom Ryan*

47

Give a man a free hand and he'll run it all over you.
Mae West (1892–1980)

I've been in more laps than a napkin.
Mae West (1892–1980)

I used to be Snow White, but I drifted.
Mae West (1892–1980)

He who hesitates is a damned fool.
Mae West (1892–1980)

I wasn't kissing her, I was whispering in her mouth.
Chico Marx (1891–1961)

Contraceptives should be used on every conceivable occasion. *From* The Last Goon Show of All

53

Bisexuality immediately doubles your chances for a date on Saturday night.   *Woody Allen*

54

What do hookers do on their nights off, type?

Elayne Boosler

55

I have perfumed my bed with myrrh, aloes, and cinnamon. Come, let us take our fill of love until the morning.   *Proverbs 7: 17–18*

56

All the men on my staff can type. *Bella Abzug*

57

A is for Apple. *Hester Prynne*

58

The perfect lover is one who turns into a pizza at 4:00 A.M. *Charles Pierce*

59

If God had meant us to have group sex, he'd have given us more organs. *Malcolm Bradbury*

60

It's been so long since I made love I can't even remember who gets tied up. *Joan Rivers*

61

Ouch! That felt good!   *Karen Elizabeth Gordon*

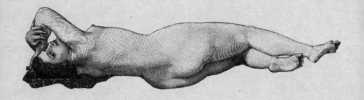

62

I never expected to see the day when girls would get
sunburned in the places they do today.

Will Rogers (1879–1935)

63

The first time we slept together she drove a recreational
vehicle into the bedroom.   *Richard Lewis*

64

A man can sleep around, no questions asked, but if a
woman makes nineteen or twenty mistakes she's a
tramp.   *Joan Rivers*

65

What do you give a man who has everything? Penicillin. *Jerry Lester*

66

Some men are so macho they'll get you pregnant just to kill a rabbit. *Maureen Murphy*

67

Chaste makes waste. *Unknown*

68

The trouble with incest is that it gets you involved with relatives. *George S. Kaufman (1889–1961)*

69

After we made love he took a piece of chalk and made an outline of my body. *Joan Rivers*

It's easy to make a friend. What's hard is to make a stranger. *Unknown*

The reason people sweat is so they won't catch fire when making love. *Don Rose*

He's such a hick he doesn't even have a trapeze in his bedroom. *Unknown*

I'm against group sex because I wouldn't know where to put my elbows. *Martin Cruz Smith*

If you want to read about love and marriage you've got to buy two separate books. *Alan King*

'Tis more blessed to give than receive; for example, wedding presents.   *H. L. Mencken (1880–1956)*

Men have a much better time of it than women; for one thing they marry later; for another thing they die earlier.   *H. L. Mencken (1880–1956)*

Monogamy is the Western custom of one wife and hardly any mistresses.

H. H. Munro (Saki) (1870–1916)

Marriage is based on the theory that when a man discovers a brand of beer exactly to his taste he should at once throw up his job and go to work in the brewery.

George Jean Nathan (1882–1958)

A wife lasts only for the length of the marriage, but an ex-wife is there *for the rest of your life.*

Jim Samuels

A man in love is incomplete until he is married. Then he is finished.   *Zsa Zsa Gabor*

A husband is what is left of the lover after the nerve has been extracted.   *Helen Rowland (1876–1950)*

When a girl marries she exchanges the attentions of many men for the inattention of one.
Helen Rowland (1876–1950)

One man's folly is another man's wife.
Helen Rowland (1876–1950)

The most happy marriage I can imagine to myself would be the union of a deaf man to a blind woman.
Samuel Taylor Coleridge (1772–1834)

The trouble with some women is that they get all excited about nothing—and then marry him.   *Cher*

Trust your husband, adore your husband, and get as much as you can in your own name.
                    Advice to Joan Rivers from her mother

Honesty has ruined more marriages than infidelity.
                    Charles McCabe (1915–1983)

Bachelors should be heavily taxed. It is not fair that some men should be happier than others.
                    Oscar Wilde (1854–1900)

I believe in the institution of marriage and I intend to keep trying until I get it right.   *Richard Pryor*

90

I was a fifty-four-year-old virgin, but I'm all right now. *Unknown*

91

Eighty percent of married men cheat in America. The rest cheat in Europe. *Jackie Mason*

A man can have two, maybe three love affairs while he's married. After that it's cheating.   *Yves Montand*

Marriage has driven more than one man to sex.
                              Peter De Vries

It destroys one's nerves to be amiable every day to the same human being.
                    Benjamin Disraeli (1804–1881)

If you are looking for a kindly, well-to-do older gentleman who is no longer interested in sex, take out an ad in *The Wall Street Journal*.
                              Abigail Van Buren

Divorce is a game played by lawyers.   *Cary Grant*

She cried, and the judge wiped her tears with my check-book.   *Tommy Manville (1894–1967)*

I can't mate in captivity.
Gloria Steinem on why she has never married

It wasn't exactly a divorce—I was traded.
Tim Conway

You don't know anything about a woman until you meet her in court.   *Norman Mailer*

I'm very old-fashioned. I believe that people should marry for life, like pigeons and Catholics.
Woody Allen

102

Marriage is like a bank account. You put it in, you take it out, you lose interest. *Professor Irwin Corey*

103

I hate babies. They're so human.
H. H. Munro (Saki) (1870–1916)

104

The baby was so ugly they had to hang a pork chop around its neck to get the dog to play with it.

Unknown

105

My mother didn't breast-feed me. She said she liked me as a friend. *Rodney Dangerfield*

106

It is no wonder that people are so horrible when they start life as children. *Kingsley Amis*

107

I was toilet-trained at gunpoint.   *Billy Braver*

108

Life does not begin at the moment of conception or the moment of birth. It begins when the kids leave home and the dog dies.   *Unknown*

109

One father is more than a hundred schoolmasters.
                    George Herbert (1593–1633)

110

An ounce of mother is worth a ton of priest.
Spanish proverb

111

Happy is the child whose father died rich.   *Proverb*

112

Reinhart was never his mother's favorite—and he was an only child.   *Thomas Berger*

113

Nature makes boys and girls lovely to look upon so they can be tolerated until they acquire some sense.
William Lyon Phelps (1865–1943)

114

The first half of our lives is ruined by our parents and the second half by our children.
Clarence Darrow (1857–1938)

Literature is mostly about having sex and not much about having children. Life is the other way around.

David Lodge

If you have never been hated by your child, you have never been a parent. *Bette Davis*

How to Raise Your I.Q. by Eating Gifted Children
Book title by Lewis B. Frumkes (1983)

Never raise your hand to your children—it leaves your midsection unprotected. *Robert Orben*

Blessed are the young, for they shall inherit the national debt. *Herbert Hoover (1874–1964)*

The denunciation of the young is a necessary part of the hygiene of older people, and greatly assists in the circulation of the blood.

Logan Pearsall Smith (1865–1946)

One of the disadvantages of having children is that they eventually get old enough to give you presents they make at school. *Robert Byrne*

Never have children, only grandchildren. *Gore Vidal*

No matter how old a mother is, she watches her middle-aged children for signs of improvement.

Florida Scott-Maxwell

Youth is such a wonderful thing. What a crime to waste it on children.

George Bernard Shaw (1856–1950)

Having children is like having a bowling alley installed in your brain. *Martin Mull*

⤳◉◉⤛

If you think education is expensive, try ignorance.
Derek Bok

I'm for bringing back the birch, but only for consenting adults. *Gore Vidal*

Education is the process of casting false pearls before real swine.   *Irwin Edman (1896–1954)*

Good teaching is one-fourth preparation and three-fourths theatre.   *Gail Godwin*

University politics are vicious precisely because the stakes are so small.   *Henry Kissinger*

Political history is far too criminal a subject to be a fit thing to teach children.

W. H. Auden (1907–1973)

I think the world is run by C students.   *Al McGuire*

Smartness runs in my family. When I went to school I was so smart my teacher was in my class for five years. *George Burns*

134

You can't expect a boy to be vicious till he's been to a good school. *H. H. Munro (Saki) (1870–1916)*

I was thrown out of college for cheating on the meta-physics exam; I looked into the soul of the boy next to me.   *Woody Allen*

❧❀❧

Beware of the man who does not drink.   *Proverb*

Water, taken in moderation, cannot hurt anybody.
Mark Twain (1835–1910)

A productive drunk is the bane of moralists.

Unknown

Come quickly, I am tasting stars!
*Dom Pérignon (1638–1715) at the
moment of his discovery of champagne*

The worst thing about some men is that when they are not drunk they are sober.

William Butler Yeats (1865–1939)

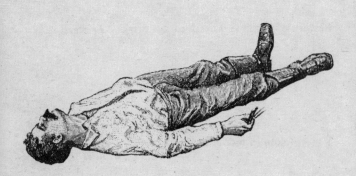

141

An Irishman is not drunk as long as he still has a blade of grass to hang onto.   *Unknown*

142

Alcohol is the anesthesia by which we endure the operation of life.   *George Bernard Shaw (1856–1950)*

143

To drink is a Christian diversion, unknown to the Turk or the Persian. *William Congreve (1670–1729)*

To one large turkey add one gallon of vermouth and a demijohn of Angostura bitters. Shake.

Recipe for turkey cocktail from
F. Scott Fitzgerald (1896–1940)

An alcoholic is someone you don't like who drinks as much as you do.   *Dylan Thomas (1914–1953)*

I can't die until the government finds a safe place to bury my liver.   *Phil Harris*

My uncle was the town drunk—and we lived in Chicago.   *George Gobel*

I've never been drunk, but often I've been overserved.

George Gobel

Somebody left the cork out of my lunch.
W. C. Fields (1880–1946)

I have to think hard to name an interesting man who does
not drink.   *Richard Burton*

I always wake up at the crack of ice.
Joe E. Lewis (1902–1971)

The graveyards are full of indispensable men.
Charles de Gaulle (1890–1970)

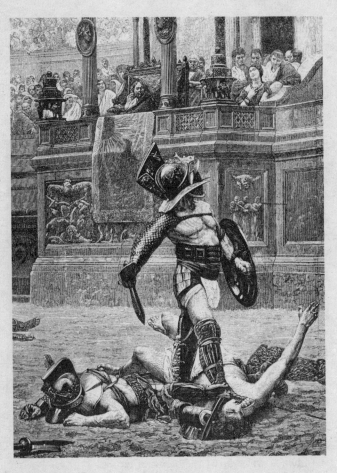

153

There are more dead people than living, and their numbers
are increasing. *Eugène Ionesco*

154

Defeat is worse than death because you have to live with
defeat. *Bill Musselman*

155

The executioner is, I hear, very expert, and my neck is
very slender. *Anne Boleyn (1507?–1536)*

156

I didn't know he was dead; I thought he was British.
Unknown

157

I believe in sex and death—two experiences that come
once in a lifetime. *Woody Allen*

158

There are worse things in life than death. Have you ever
spent an evening with an insurance salesman?
Woody Allen

Go away. I'm all right.
Last words of H. G. Wells (1885–1946)

⋙◉⋘

You can pretend to be serious; you can't pretend to be witty. *Sacha Guitry (1885–1957)*

Everybody likes a kidder, but nobody lends him money. *Arthur Miller*

One doesn't have a sense of humor. It has you.
Larry Gelbart

The aim of a joke is not to degrade the human being but to remind him that he is already degraded.
George Orwell (1903–1950)

164

If you don't count some of Jehovah's injunctions, there are no humorists in the Bible. *Mordecai Richler*

165

Dying is easy. Comedy is difficult.
Actor Edmond Gwenn (1875–1959)
on his deathbed

166

Humorists always sit at the children's table.
Woody Allen

167

I don't care where I sit as long as I get fed.
Calvin Trillin

168

What is comedy? Comedy is the art of making people laugh without making them puke. *Steve Martin*

ↄ⊚⊙⊙ↄ

Until Eve arrived, this was a man's world.

Richard Armour

170

Whatever women do they must do twice as well as men to be thought half as good. Luckily, this is not difficult. *Charlotte Whitton (1896–1975)*

171

Don't accept rides from strange men, and remember that all men are strange. *Robin Morgan*

172

There are only two kinds of men—the dead and the deadly. *Helen Rowland (1876–1950)*

173

Men are creatures with two legs and eight hands.
Jayne Mansfield (1932–1967)

174

I refuse to consign the whole male sex to the nursery. I insist on believing that some men are my equals.
Brigid Brophy

175

Being a woman is a terribly difficult trade, since it consists principally of dealing with men.
Joseph Conrad (1857–1924)

Being a woman is of special interest to aspiring male trans-
sexuals. To actual women it is simply a good excuse not
to play football.   *Fran Lebowitz*

My advice to the women's clubs of America is to raise
more hell and fewer dahlias.
                    William Allen White (1868–1944)

A lady is one who never shows her underwear uninten-
tionally.   *Lillian Day*

Anyone who says he can see through women is missing
a lot.   *Groucho Marx (1895–1977)*

The most popular labor-saving device today is still a husband with money.   *Joey Adams*

181

A gentleman never strikes a lady with his hat on.
Fred Allen (1894–1956)

182

I've never struck a woman in my life, not even my own mother. *W. C. Fields (1880–1946)*

183

If you become a star, *you* don't change, everyone else does. *Kirk Douglas*

184

I'm not a real movie star—I've still got the same wife I started out with twenty-eight years ago.
Will Rogers (1879–1935)

185

Fame lost its appeal for me when I went into a public restroom and an autograph seeker handed me a pen and paper under the stall door. *Marlo Thomas*

186

If I had done everything I'm credited with, I'd be speaking to you from a laboratory jar at Harvard.

Frank Sinatra

187

AS USUAL, YOUR INFORMATION STINKS.

Telegram to Time *magazine from Frank Sinatra*

188

As an anti-American, I thank you for your rotten article devoted to my person.

Letter to Time *magazine from Prince Sihanouk*

189

I am a deeply superficial person.   *Andy Warhol*

190

I have bursts of being a lady, but it doesn't last long.

Shelley Winters

Working with Julie Andrews is like getting hit over the head with a valentine.   *Christopher Plummer*

I should have been a country-western singer. After all, I'm older than most western countries.

George Burns

Never face facts; if you do you'll never get up in the morning.   *Marlo Thomas*

⋐◉⊕◉⋑

Nothing succeeds like the appearance of success.

Christopher Lasch

She's the kind of girl who climbed the ladder of success wrong by wrong.   *Mae West (1892–1980)*

196

Nothing fails like success.   *Gerald Nachman*

197

Anyone seen on a bus after the age of thirty has been a failure in life.   *Loelia, Duchess of Westminster*

198

To err is human
And stupid.

Robert Byrne

199

You may already be a loser.
Form letter received by Rodney Dangerfield

200

How should they answer?
*Abigail Van Buren in reply to the question
"Why do Jews always answer a question
with a question?"*

201

If you live in New York, even if you're Catholic, you're Jewish. *Lenny Bruce (1923–1966)*

202

Jews always know two things: suffering and where to find great Chinese food.
From the movie My Favorite Year, *1982*

203

The goys have proven the following theorem....
Physicist John von Neumann (1903–1957)
at the start of a classroom lecture

204

I want to be the white man's brother, not his brother-in-law. *Martin Luther King, Jr. (1929–1968)*

205

I have just enough white in me to make my honesty questionable. *Will Rogers (1879–1935)*

206

I never believed in Santa Claus because I knew no white dude would come into my neighborhood after dark.

Dick Gregory

❧⊙H⊙❧

207

Work is of two kinds: first, altering the position of matter at or near the earth's surface relative to other matter; second, telling other people to do so.

Bertrand Russell (1872–1970)

All jobs should be open to everybody, unless they actually require a penis or vagina.

Florynce Kennedy

It is impossible to enjoy idling unless there is plenty of work to do. *Jerome K. Jerome (1859–1927)*

Anybody who works is a fool. I don't work, I merely inflict myself on the public. *Robert Morley*

Hard work never killed anybody, but why take a chance?
Charlie McCarthy (Edgar Bergen, 1903–1978)

If you have a job without aggravations, you don't have a job. *Malcolm Forbes*

People who work sitting down get paid more than people who work standing up.

Ogden Nash (1902–1971)

Work is much more fun than fun.

Noel Coward (1899–1973)

The trouble with the rat race is that even if you win you're still a rat. *Lily Tomlin*

Money is good for bribing yourself through the inconveniences of life. *Gottfried Reinhardt*

A billion here, a billion there—pretty soon it adds up to real money.

Senator Everett Dirksen (1896–1969)

218

I have enough money to last me the rest of my life, unless I buy something. *Jackie Mason*

219

The rich have a passion for bargains as lively as it is pointless. *Françoise Sagan*

220

Whoever said money can't buy happiness didn't know where to shop. *Unknown*

221

Behind every great fortune there is a crime.
Honoré de Balzac (1799–1850)

222

The richer your friends, the more they will cost you.
Elisabeth Marbury (1856–1933)

223

Money is always there, but the pockets change.
                           Gertrude Stein (1874–1946)

224

There must be more to life than having everything.
                           Maurice Sendak

225

If women didn't exist, all the money in the world would
have no meaning.
                           Aristotle Onassis (1906–1975)

226

Better to be nouveau than never to have been riche at
all.   *Unknown*

227

Save a little money each month and at the end of the year
you'll be surprised at how little you have.
                           Ernest Haskins

228

My problem lies in reconciling my gross habits with my net income.   *Errol Flynn (1909–1959)*

229

Any man who has $10,000 left when he dies is a failure.   *Errol Flynn (1909–1959)*

230

The wages of sin are unreported.   *Unknown*

231

I'm living so far beyond my income that we may almost be said to be living apart.

e e cummings (1894–1962)

232

To get back on your feet, miss two car payments.

Unknown

233

When I first arrived in this country I had only fifteen cents in my pocket and a willingness to compromise.

Weber cartoon caption

⦿

234

Fashion is a form of ugliness so intolerable that we have to alter it every six months.

Oscar Wilde (1856–1900)

235

If you look good and dress well, you don't need a purpose in life. *Fashion consultant Robert Pante*

Every generation laughs at the old fashions but religiously follows the new.

Henry David Thoreau (1817–1862)

I base my fashion taste on what doesn't itch.

Gilda Radner

War is a series of catastrophes that results in a victory. *Georges Clemenceau (1841–1929)*

You can no more win a war than you can win an earthquake. *Jeannette Rankin (1880–1973)*

I'd like to see the government get out of war altogether and leave the whole field to private industry.

Joseph Heller

The object of war is not to die for your country but to make the other bastard die for his.

General George Patton (1885–1945)

242

Name me an emperor who was ever struck by a cannon-ball. *Charles V (1500–1558)*

243

While you're saving your face you're losing your ass.

President Lyndon Johnson (1908–1973)

244

You can't say civilization don't advance ... in every war they kill you a new way.

Will Rogers (1879–1935)

I have already given two cousins to the war and I stand
ready to sacrifice my wife's brother.

Artemus Ward (1834–1867)

Join the army, see the world, meet interesting people, and
kill them.   *Unknown*

Being in the army is like being in the Boy Scouts, except
that the Boy Scouts have adult supervision.

Blake Clark

The Israelis are the Doberman pinschers of the Middle
East. They treat the Arabs like postmen.

Franklyn Ajaye

PART TWO

Advice
Health
Food
Life Itself
America
Psychoses
Books
Writers
Music
Show Business
Animals
Doctors
Presidents
Politics
Sports
and much else

Start slow and taper off.   *Walt Stack*

Never get into fights with ugly people because they have nothing to lose.   *Unknown*

Never miss a good chance to shut up.
                              Scott Beach's grandfather

The best way to keep one's word is not to give it.
                              Napoleon (1769–1821)

It's all right letting yourself go as long as you can let yourself back.   *Mick Jagger*

254

Sometimes a scream is better than a thesis.
Ralph Waldo Emerson (1803–1882)

255

Aaeeeyaaayaaayaayaa...
Johnny Weissmuller (1904–1984)

256

When walking through a melon patch, don't adjust your sandals. *Chinese proverb*

257

Sometimes a fool makes a good suggestion.
Nicolas Boileau (1636–1711)

258

Good advice is one of those insults that ought to be forgiven. *Unknown*

✥⊙⊦⊙✥

259

It's no longer a question of staying healthy. It's a question of finding a sickness you like.   *Jackie Mason*

260

I've just learned about his illness. Let's hope it's nothing trivial.   *Variously ascribed*

261

I don't deserve this award, but I have arthritis and I don't deserve that either.   *Jack Benny (1894–1974)*

262

As for me, except for an occasional heart attack, I feel as young as I ever did.

Robert Benchley (1889–1945)

263

I get my exercise acting as a pallbearer to my friends who exercise.   *Chauncey Depew (1834–1928)*

264

Avoid running at all time.

Satchel Paige (1906?–1982)

265

It is more profitable for your congressman to support the tobacco industry than your life.   *Jackie Mason*

266

Smoking is one of the leading causes of statistics.

Fletcher Knebel

267

Quit worrying about your health. It'll go away.

Robert Orben

268

Health nuts are going to feel stupid someday, lying in hospitals dying of nothing.   *Redd Foxx*

❧⊗❧

269

To eat is human
To digest divine.

Mark Twain (1835–1910)

270

There is no sincerer love than the love of food.

George Bernard Shaw (1856–1950)

271

The most dangerous food is wedding cake.

American proverb

272

Roumanian-Yiddish cooking has killed more Jews than Hitler. *Zero Mostel (1915–1977)*

273

I believe that eating pork makes people stupid.

David Steinberg

Eat, drink, and be merry, for tomorrow we may diet.
Unknown

275

When men reach their sixties and retire, they go to pieces.
Women go right on cooking.   *Gail Sheehy*

276

I've been on a diet for two weeks and all I've lost is two
weeks.   *Totie Fields (1931–1978)*

I'm on a seafood diet. I see food and I eat it.

Variously ascribed

Eat as much as you like—just don't swallow it.

Harry Secombe's diet

Put a pot of chili on the stove to simmer.
Let it simmer. Meanwhile, broil a good steak.
Eat the steak. Let the chili simmer. Ignore it.

*Recipe for chili from Allan Shivers,
former governor of Texas*

The two biggest sellers in any bookstore are the cookbooks and the diet books. The cookbooks tell you how to prepare the food and the diet books tell you how not to eat any of it. *Andy Rooney*

It's so beautifully arranged on the plate—you know someone's fingers have been all over it.

Julia Child on nouvelle cuisine

282

A gourmet who thinks of calories is like a tart who looks at her watch.   *James Beard*

283

Where do you go to get anorexia?   *Shelley Winters*

284

Nachman's Rule: When it comes to foreign food, the less authentic the better.   *Gerald Nachman*

285

I eat merely to put food out of my mind.

N. F. Simpson

286

Isn't there any other part of the matzo you can eat?
*Marilyn Monroe (1926–1962) on being
served matzo ball soup three meals in a row*

287

A gourmet restaurant in Cincinnati is one where you leave the tray on the table after you eat.   *Unknown*

288

When compelled to cook, I produce a meal that would make a sword swallower gag.   *Russell Baker*

289

Poets have been mysteriously silent on the subject of cheese.   *G. K. Chesterton (1874–1936)*

290

I don't even butter my bread. I consider that cooking.
Katherine Cebrian

291

Life is too short to stuff a mushroom. *Storm Jameson*

292

The most remarkable thing about my mother is that for thirty years she served the family nothing but leftovers. The original meal has never been found.
Calvin Trillin

293

I'm in favor of liberalized immigration because of the effect it would have on restaurants. I'd let just about everybody in except the English.
Calvin Trillin

294

No man is lonely while eating spaghetti.
Robert Morley

I prefer my oysters fried;
That way I know my oysters died.
                    Roy G. Blount, Jr.

296
The trouble with life in the fast lane is that you get to the
other end in an awful hurry. *John Jensen*

297

It is not true that life is one damn thing after another—
it is one damn thing over and over.

Edna St. Vincent Millay (1892–1950)

298

Life is thirst. *Leonard Michaels*

299

The less things change, the more they remain the
same. *Sicilian proverb*

300

There are days when it takes all you've got just to keep
up with the losers. *Robert Orben*

301

If you can see the light at the end of the tunnel you are
looking the wrong way. *Barry Commoner*

302

I have found little that is good about human beings.
In my experience most of them are trash.

Sigmund Freud (1856–1939)

303

The brotherhood of man is not a mere poet's dream; it is
a most depressing and humiliating reality.

Oscar Wilde (1854–1900)

304

We're all in this alone. *Lily Tomlin*

305

Our ignorance of history makes us libel our own times.
People have always been like this.

Gustave Flaubert (1821–1880)

306

The British tourist is always happy abroad so long as the
natives are waiters. *Robert Morley*

307

You can't judge Egypt by *Aïda*. *Ronald Firbank*

308

France is a country where the money falls apart and you can't tear the toilet paper. *Billy Wilder*

309

In Marseilles they make half the toilet soap we consume in America, but the Marseillaise only have a vague theoretical idea of its use, which they have obtained from books of travel.

Mark Twain (1835–1910)

310

Gaiety is the most outstanding feature of the Soviet Union. *Joseph Stalin (1879–1953)*

311

In Italy, for thirty years under the Borgias, they had warfare, terror, murder, and bloodshed, but they produced Michelangelo, Leonardo da Vinci, and the Renaissance. In Switzerland, they had brotherly love, they had five hundred years of democracy and peace—and what did they produce? The cuckoo clock.

From the movie The Third Man, *1949*

Canada is so square even the female impersonators are women.   *From the movie* Outrageous, *1983*

Most Texans think Hanukkah is some sort of duck call.
                                                    Richard Lewis

Historians have now definitely established that Juan Cabrillo, discoverer of California, was not looking for Kansas, thus setting a precedent that continues to this day.   *Wayne Shannon*

The big cities of America are becoming Third World countries.   *Nora Ephron*

New York now leads the world's great cities in the number of people around whom you shouldn't make a sudden move.   *David Letterman*

317

It isn't necessary to have relatives in Kansas City in order to be unhappy. *Groucho Marx (1895–1977)*

318

Isn't it nice that people who prefer Los Angeles to San Francisco live there? *Herb Caen*

319

San Francisco is like granola: Take away the fruits and the nuts, and all you have are the flakes.

Unknown

320

In San Francisco, Halloween is redundant.

Will Durst

321

Detroit is Cleveland without the glitter. *Unknown*

When I saw a sign on the freeway that said, "Los Angeles 445 miles," I said to myself, "I've got to get out of this lane." *Franklyn Ajaye*

323

Traffic signals in New York are just rough guidelines.
David Letterman

324

I have an existential map. It has "You are here" written all over it.   *Steven Wright*

325

I hate small towns because once you've seen the cannon in the park there's nothing else to do.
Lenny Bruce (1923–1966)

326

Schizophrenia beats dining alone.   *Unknown*

327

When we talk to God, we're praying. When God talks to us, we're schizophrenic.   *Lily Tomlin*

328

When dealing with the insane, the best method is to pretend to be sane.   *Hermann Hesse (1877–1962)*

329

I don't really trust a sane person.
                    Pro football lineman Lyle Alzado

330

Sometimes when you look in his eyes you get the feeling that someone else is driving.   *David Letterman*

331

I'm going to give my psychoanalyst one more year, then I'm going to Lourdes.   *Woody Allen*

❦

332

When a book and a head collide and there is a hollow sound, is it always from the book?
                    Georg Christoph Lichtenberg (1742–1799)

333

I've given up reading books. I find it takes my mind off myself.   *Oscar Levant (1906–1972)*

334

Where do I find the time for not reading so many books? *Karl Kraus (1874–1936)*

335

A person who publishes a book appears willfully in public with his pants down.
Edna St. Vincent Millay (1892–1950)

336

The reason why so few good books are written is that so few people who can write know anything.
Walter Bagehot (1826–1877)

337

The newspaper is the natural enemy of the book, as the whore is of the decent woman.
The Goncourt Brothers, 1858

338

Manuscript: Something submitted in haste and returned at leisure.   *Oliver Herford (1863–1935)*

339

Your manuscript is both good and original, but the part that is good is not original and the part that is original is not good.   *Samuel Johnson (1709–1784)*

340

Autobiography is an unrivaled vehicle for telling the truth about other people.

Philip Guedalla (1889–1944)

341

A well-written life is almost as rare as a well-spent one.   *Thomas Carlyle (1795–1881)*

342

I have read your book and much like it.

Moses Hadas (1900–1966)

343

A novel is a piece of prose of a certain length with something wrong with it.   *Unknown*

344

There are two kinds of books: those that no one reads and those that no one ought to read.
H. L. Mencken (1880–1956)

345

The covers of this book are too far apart.
Ambrose Bierce (1842–1914?)

346

[He] took me into his library and showed me his books, of which he had a complete set.
Ring Lardner (1885–1933)

347

The man who reads nothing at all is better educated than the man who reads nothing but newspapers.
Thomas Jefferson (1743–1826)

Journalism largely consists in saying "Lord Jones is dead" to people who never knew Lord Jones was alive.

G. K. Chesterton (1874–1936)

There is so much to be said in favor of modern journalism. By giving us the opinions of the uneducated it keeps us in touch with ignorance of the community.

Oscar Wilde (1854–1900)

Small Earthquake in Chile;
Not Many Killed

Headline suggested for The Times
of London by Claud Cockburn

Writers have two main problems. One is writer's block, when the words won't come at all, and the other is logorrhea, when the words come so fast that they can hardly get to the wastebasket in time.

Cecilia Bartholomew

All of us learn to write in the second grade. Most of us go on to greater things.

Basketball coach Bobby Knight

When writers refer to themselves as "we" and to the reader as "you," it's two against one.   *Judith Rascoe*

Most writers regard the truth as their most valuable possession, and therefore are most economical in its use.   *Mark Twain (1835–1910)*

Writing is turning one's worst moments into money.

J. P. Donleavy

Writing is the only profession in which one can make no money without being ridiculous.

Jules Renard (1864–1910)

Writers should be read, but neither seen nor heard.
Daphne Du Maurier

If you can't annoy somebody, there is little point in writing.   *Kingsley Amis*

Unprovided with original learning, unformed in the habits of thinking, unskilled in the arts of composition, I resolved to write a book.

Edward Gibbon (1737–1794)

Everywhere I go I'm asked if I think the university stifles writers. My opinion is that they don't stifle enough of them. There's many a bestseller that could have been prevented by a good teacher.

Flannery O'Connor (1925–1964)

Great Moments in Literature: In 1936, Ernest Hemingway, while trout fishing, caught a carp and decided not to write about it.   *Guindon cartoon caption*

All writing is garbage.
French playwright Antonin Artaud (1896–1948)

Novelists who go to psychiatrists are paying for what they should be paid for. *Unknown*

Every author, however modest, keeps a most outrageous vanity chained like a madman in the padded cell of his breast. *Logan Pearsall Smith (1865–1946)*

The trouble with our younger writers is that they are all in their sixties.
W. Somerset Maugham (1874–1965)

366

Authors are easy to get on with—if you like children.

Michael Joseph (1897–1958)

367

I write fiction because it's a way of making statements I
can disown, and I write plays because dialogue is the most
respectable way of contradicting myself.

Tom Stoppard

368

An essayist is a lucky person who has found a way to discourse without being interrupted. *Charles Poore*

369

Writers aren't exactly people...they're a whole lot of people trying to be one person.
F. Scott Fitzgerald (1896–1940)

370

An author's first duty is to let down his country.
Brendan Behan (1923–1964)

371

Asking a working writer what he thinks about critics is like asking a lamp-post how it feels about dogs.
Christopher Hampton

372

I can't read ten pages of Steinbeck without throwing up. *James Gould Cozzens (1903–1978)*

373

A poem is never finished, only abandoned.
Paul Valéry (1871–1945)

374

Immature poets imitate; mature poets steal.
T. S. Eliot (1888–1965)

375

Good swiping is an art in itself.   *Jules Feiffer*

376

Finishing a book is just like you took a child out in the back yard and shot it.   *Truman Capote*

377

Dear Contributor: Thank you for not sending us anything lately. It suits our present needs.
Note from publisher received by Snoopy in comic strip "Peanuts" (Charles Schulz)

378

You call this a script? Give me a couple of 5,000-dollar-a-week writers and I'll write it myself.

Movie producer Joe Pasternak

379

I do most of my writing sitting down. That's where I shine.   *Robert Benchley (1889–1945)*

380

When in doubt, have two guys come through the door with guns.   *Raymond Chandler (1888–1959)*

381

Too many pieces of music finish too long after the end.   *Igor Stravinsky (1882–1971)*

382

My music is best understood by children and animals.
Igor Stravinsky (1882–1971)

383

You want something by Bach? Which one, Johann Sebastian or Jacques Offen? *Victor Borge*

Even Bach comes down to the basic suck, blow, suck, suck, blow. *Mouth organist Larry Adler*

Classical music is the kind we keep thinking will turn into a tune. *Kin Hubbard (1868–1930)*

Opera in English is, in the main, just about as sensible as baseball in Italian. *H. L. Mencken (1880–1956)*

387

I tried to resist his overtures, but he plied me with symphonies, quartettes, chamber music, and cantatas.

S. J. Perelman (1904–1979)

388

Anything that is too stupid to be spoken is sung.

Voltaire (1694–1778)

389

Massenet
Never wrote a Mass in A.
It'd have been just too bad
If he had.

Anthony Butts

390

No statue has ever been put up to a critic.

Jean Sibelius (1865–1957)

391

Music played at weddings always reminds me of the music played for soldiers before they go into battle.

Heinrich Heine (1797–1856)

I don't know anything about music. In my line you don't have to. *Elvis Presley (1935–1977)*

393

Hell is full of musical amateurs.
George Bernard Shaw (1856–1950)

394

No sane man will dance. *Cicero (106–43* B.C.)

Rock and roll is the hamburger that ate the world.

Peter York

396

Use an accordion, go to jail! That's the law!

Bumper sticker

You can make a killing as a playwright in America, but you can't make a living.

Sherwood Anderson (1876–1941)

All playwrights should be dead for three hundred years. *Joseph L. Mankiewicz*

Actresses will happen in the best regulated families.

Oliver Herford (1863–1935)

My tears stuck in their little ducts, refusing to be jerked. *Peter Stack in a movie review*

His performance is so wooden you want to spray him with Liquid Pledge. *John Stark in a movie review*

Working in the theater has a lot in common with unemployment.   *Arthur Gingold*

Only in show business could a guy with a C-minus average be considered an intellectual.

Mort Sahl on himself

I don't want to see the uncut version of anything.

Jean Kerr

It's always easier to see a show you don't like the second time because you know it ends.

Walter Slezak (1902–1983)

Hell is a half-filled auditorium.

Robert Frost (1874–1963)

407

A critic is a man who knows the way but can't drive the car.   *Kenneth Tynan (1927–1980)*

408

Hollywood is a place where they place you under contract instead of under observation.
Walter Winchell (1897–1972)

409

The Hollywood tradition I like best is called "sucking up to the stars."   *Johnny Carson*

410

"Hello," he lied.
Don Carpenter quoting a Hollywood agent

411

An associate producer is the only guy in Hollywood who will associate with a producer.
Fred Allen (1894–1956)

The dead actor requested in his will that his body be cremated and ten percent of his ashes thrown in his agent's face. *Unknown*

It was like passing the scene of a highway accident and being relieved to learn that nobody had been seriously injured.

> *Martin Cruz Smith on being asked how he liked*
> *the movie version of his novel* Gorky Park

If you want to make it in show business, get the hell out of Oregon.

> *Advice from Sophie Tucker (1884–1966)*
> *to a young Johnnie Ray*

Television has proved that people will look at anything rather than each other. *Ann Landers*

Television is more interesting than people. If it were not, we would have people standing in the corners of our rooms. *Alan Corenk*

Television is a medium because anything well done is rare.
Either Fred Allen (1894–1956)
or Ernie Kovacs (1919–1962)

Your picture tube is okay, but your cabinet has Dutch elm disease.   *TV repairman in a Ziggy cartoon*

I'm So Miserable Without You
It's Almost Like Having You Here
Stephen Bishop song title

She Got the Gold Mine, I Got the Shaft
Jerry Reed song title

When My Love Comes Back from the Ladies' Room Will I Be Too Old to Care?
Lewis Grizzard song title

422

I Don't Know Whether to Kill Myself or Go Bowling
Song title by Unknown

423

Why won't you lemme feelya, Cecilia?
I got two winnin' hands I wanna dealya.
Lyrics by Robert Byrne

424

They Tore Out My Heart and Stomped That Sucker
Flat   *Book title by Lewis Grizzard*

❧⊙❧

425

[Americans] are a race of convicts and ought to be thankful for anything we allow them short of hanging.
Samuel Johnson (1709–1784)

426

America is a large friendly dog in a small room. Every time it wags its tail it knocks over a chair.
Arnold Toynbee (1889–1975)

The United States is like the guy at the party who gives cocaine to everybody and still nobody likes him.

Jim Samuels

428

In America there are two classes of travel—first and with children. *Robert Benchley (1889–1945)*

On Thanksgiving Day all over America, families sit down
to dinner at the same moment—halftime.

Unknown

&⊙H⊙&

Animals have these advantages over man: they never hear
the clock strike, they die without any idea of death, they
have no theologians to instruct them, their last moments
are not disturbed by unwelcome and unpleasant cere-
monies, their funerals cost them nothing, and no one starts
lawsuits over their wills.

Voltaire (1694–1778)

A boy can learn a lot from a dog: obedience, loyalty, and
the importance of turning around three times before lying
down. *Robert Benchley (1889–1945)*

Man is the only animal that can remain on friendly terms
with the victims he intends to eat until he eats
them. *Samuel Butler (1835–1902)*

Fox hunting is the unspeakable in pursuit of the inedi-
ble. *Oscar Wilde (1856–1900)*

434

If you are a police dog, where's your badge?
The question James Thurber (1894–1961)
used to drive his German shepherd crazy

435

I loathe people who keep dogs. They are cowards who haven't got the guts to bite people themselves.
August Strindberg (1849–1912)

436

People on horses look better than they are, people in cars look worse. *Marya Mannes*

437

We tolerate shapes in human beings that would horrify us if we saw them in a horse.

W. R. Inge (1860–1954)

438

You're a good example of why some animals eat their young.   *Jim Samuels to a heckler*

439

Cats are intended to teach us that not everything in nature has a function.   *Garrison Keillor*

440

Groundhog Day has been observed only once in Los Angeles because when the groundhog came out of its hole, it was killed by a mud slide.   *Johnny Carson*

441

Is that a beard, or are you eating a muskrat?

Dr. Gonzo

442

To err is human
To purr feline.

Robert Byrne

443

It isn't easy being green. *Kermit the Frog*

444

Never go to a doctor whose office plants have died.
Erma Bombeck

445

Three out of four doctors recommend another doctor.
Graffito

446

I suppose one has a greater sense of intellectual degradation after an interview with a doctor than from any human experience. *Alice James (1848–1892)*

447

A young doctor means a new graveyard.

German proverb

448

I'm going to Boson to see my doctor. He's a very sick man.   *Fred Allen (1894–1956)*

449

People who take cold baths never have rheumatism, but they have cold baths.   *Unknown*

450

His ideas of first-aid stopped short of squirting soda water.   *P. G. Wodehouse (1881–1975)*

451

Before undergoing a surgical operation, arrange your temporal affairs. You may live.

Ambrose Bierce (1842–1914?)

452

Psychoanalysis is that mental illness for which it regards itself a therapy.   *Karl Kraus (1874–1936)*

453

Show me a sane man and I will cure him for you.

C. G. Jung (1875–1961)

454

Psychiatry is the care of the id by the odd.   *Unknown*

455

After twelve years of therapy my psychiatrist said something that brought tears to my eyes. He said, "*No hablo inglés.*"   *Ronnie Shakes*

456

Doctors and lawyers must go to school for years and years, often with little sleep and with great sacrifice to their first wives.   *Roy G. Blount, Jr.*

457

I never did give anybody hell. I just told the truth and they thought it was hell.

Harry S Truman (1884–1972)

458

I can think of nothing more boring for the American people than to have to sit in their living rooms for a whole half hour looking at my face on their television screens.   *Dwight David Eisenhower (1890–1969)*

459

Do you realize the responsibility I carry? I'm the only person standing between Nixon and the White House.
John F. Kennedy (1917–1963), in 1960

460

I'm not sure I've even got the brains to be President.
Barry Goldwater in 1964

461

I would not like to be a political leader in Russia. They never know when they're being taped.

Richard Nixon

462

I love America. You always hurt the one you love.
David Frye impersonating Nixon

The thought of being President frightens me and I do not think I want the job.   *Ronald Reagan in 1973*

God! The country that produced George Washington has got this collection of crumb-bums!
*Barbara Tuchman on the 1980
presidential candidates*

Reagan won because he ran against Jimmy Carter. Had he run unopposed he would have lost.   *Mort Sahl*

Ronald Reagan is a triumph of the embalmer's art.
Gore Vidal

Ronald Reagan's platform seems to be: Hey, I'm a big good-looking guy and I need a lot of sleep.
Roy G. Blount, Jr.

468

Walter Mondale has all the charisma of a speed bump.
Will Durst

469

You've got to be careful quoting Ronald Reagan, because when you quote him accurately it's called mudslinging.   *Walter Mondale*

470

Women are being considered as candidates for Vice President of the United States because it is the worst job in America. It's amazing that men will take it. A job with real power is First Lady. I'd be willing to run for that. As far as the men who are running for President are concerned, they aren't even people I would date.
Nora Ephron

471

The man with the best job in the country is the Vice President. All he has to do is get up every morning and say, "How's the President?"
Will Rogers (1879–1935)

472

The vice-presidency ain't worth a pitcher of warm spit.
Vice President John Nance Garner (1868–1967)

If it were not for the government, we would have nothing to laugh at in France.

Sébastian Chamfort (1740–1794)

Every decent man is ashamed of the government he lives under. *H. L. Mencken (1880–1956)*

It has been said that democracy is the worst form of government except all the others that have been tried.

Winston Churchill (1874–1965)

Democracy substitutes election by the incompetent many for appointment by the corrupt few.

George Bernard Shaw (1856–1950)

Get all the fools on your side and you can be elected to anything. *Frank Dane*

If voting changed anything, they'd make it illegal.
Unknown

Vote early and vote often.   *Al Capone (1899–1947)*

Ninety percent of the politicians give the other ten percent a bad reputation.   *Henry Kissinger*

Politics is applesauce.   *Will Rogers (1879–1935)*

I might have gone to West Point, but I was too proud to speak to a congressman.   *Will Rogers (1879–1935)*

An ambassador is an honest man sent abroad to lie for his country.   *Sir Henry Wotton (1568–1639)*

A statesman is a politician who has been dead ten or fifteen years.   *Harry S Truman (1884–1972)*

Right in the middle of Prague, Wenceslaus Square, there's this guy throwing up. And this other guy comes along, takes a look at him, shakes his head, and says, "I know just what you mean."   *Milan Kundera*

When you go into court you are putting your fate into the hands of twelve people who weren't smart enough to get out of jury duty.   *Norm Crosby*

Getting kicked out of the American Bar Association is like getting kicked out of the Book-of-the-Month Club.
*Melvin Belli on the occasion of his getting
kicked out of the American Bar Association*

488

Laws are like sausages. It's better not to see them being made.   *Otto von Bismarck (1815–1898)*

❧◉❧

489

I always turn to the sports pages first, which record people's accomplishments. The front page has nothing but man's failures.
Chief Justice Earl Warren (1891–1974)

490

I was not successful as a ballplayer, as it was a game of skill.   *Casey Stengel (1891–1975)*

491

It matters not whether you win or lose; what matters is whether *I* win or lose.   *Darrin Weinberg*

492

I'm glad we don't have to play in the shade.
Golfer Bobby Jones (1902–1971) on being told that it was 105 degrees in the shade

Very few blacks will take up golf until the requirement for plaid pants is dropped.   *Franklyn Ajaye*

San Francisco has always been my favorite booing city. I don't mean the people boo louder or longer, but there is a very special intimacy. When they boo you, you know they mean *you*. Music, that's what it is to me. One time in Kezar Stadium they gave me a standing boo.
                    Pro football coach George Halas (1895–1983)

Most weightlifters are biceptual.   *John Rostoni*

I never met a man I didn't want to fight.
                    Pro football lineman Lyle Alzado

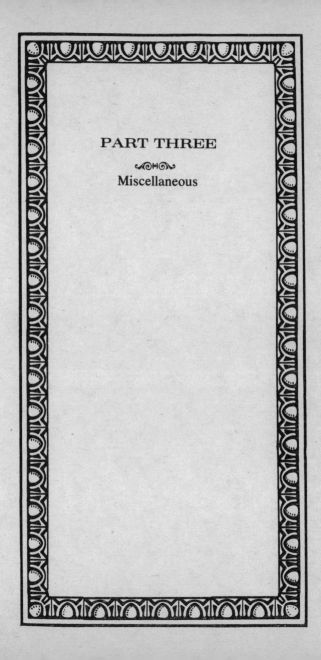

PART THREE

Miscellaneous

If politicians and scientists were lazier, how much happier we should all be.

Evelyn Waugh (1903–1966)

If we see the light at the end of the tunnel
It's the light of an oncoming train.

Robert Lowell (1917–1977)

Ninety percent of everything is crap.

Theodore Sturgeon

You've always made the mistake of being yourself.

Eugène Ionesco

There is such a build-up of crud in my oven there is only room to bake a single cupcake. *Phyllis Diller*

Cleaning your house while your kids are still growing is
like shoveling the walk before it stops snowing.
Phyllis Diller

503
All phone calls are obscene. *Karen Elizabeth Gordon*

504

There is no need to do any housework at all. After the first four years the dirt doesn't get any worse.

Quentin Crisp

505

Coincidences are spiritual puns.

G. K. Chesterton (1874–1936)

506

If I had to live my life again, I'd make the same mistakes, only sooner.

Tallulah Bankhead (1903–1968)

507

Last night I dreamed I ate a ten-pound marshmallow, and when I woke up the pillow was gone.

Tommy Cooper

508

It's better to be wanted for murder than not to be wanted at all. *Marty Winch*

I have a hundred times wished that one could resign life as an officer resigns a commission.
Robert Burns (1759–1796)

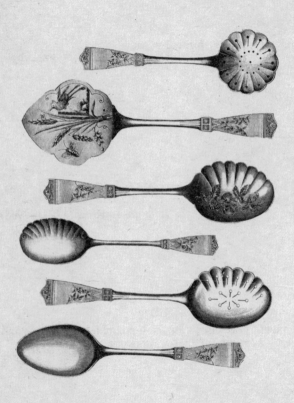

The more he talked of his honor the faster we counted our spoons. *Ralph Waldo Emerson (1803–1882)*

511

If you tell the truth you don't have to remember anything.   *Mark Twain (1835–1910)*

512

The truth is the safest lie.   *Anonymous*

513

No one can have a higher opinion of him than I have, and I think he's a dirty little beast.

W. S. Gilbert (1836–1911)

514

The future is much like the present, only longer.

Don Quisenberry

515

Advertising is the rattling of a stick inside a swill bucket.   *George Orwell (1903–1950)*

516

Winter is nature's way of saying, "Up yours."
Robert Byrne

517

I like winter because I can stay indoors without feeling guilty. *Teressa Skelton*

518

Weather forecast for tonight: dark. *George Carlin*

519

If I were two-faced, would I be wearing this one?
Abraham Lincoln (1809–1865)

520

A person can take only so much comforting.
Calvin Trillir

521

I have a rock garden. Last week three of them died.
Richard Diran

522

Nice guys finish last, but we get to sleep in.
Evan Davis

523

Illegal aliens have always been a problem in the United States. Ask any Indian.   *Robert Orben*

524

Few things are harder to put up with than a good example.   *Mark Twain (1835–1910)*

525

I just got wonderful news from my real estate agent in Florida. They found land on my property.
Milton Berle

526

Immigration is the sincerest form of flattery.   *Jack Paar*

527

The art of living is more like wrestling than dancing.
Marcus Aurelius (121–180)

528

We must believe in luck. For how else can we explain the success of those we don't like?
Jean Cocteau (1889–1963)

529

Hell is other people.   *Jean Paul Sartre (1905–1980)*

530

Some people are always late, like the late King George V.

Spike Milligan

531

It is easier to get forgiveness than permission.
*Stewart's Law of Retroaction
in* Murphy's Law, Book Two

532

The popularity of a bad man is as treacherous as he is himself.   *Pliny the Younger (c. 62–c. 113)*

533

The hatred of relatives is the most violent.
Tacitus (c.55–c. 117)

534

Every man sees in his relatives a series of grotesque caricatures of himself.   *H. L. Mencken (1880–1956)*

535

The first Rotarian was the first man to call John the Baptist "Jack."   *H. L. Mencken (1880–1956)*

536

Even if you're on the right track, you'll get run over if you just sit there.   *Will Rogers (1879–1935)*

H. L. Mencken suffers from the hallucination that he is
H. L. Mencken. There is no cure for a disease of that
magnitude. *Maxwell Bodenhein (1893–1954)*

I prefer rogues to imbeciles because they sometimes take
a rest.

Alexandre Dumas the Younger (1824–1895)

A wedding cake left out in the rain.

*Stephen Spender commenting on the face of
W. H. Auden (1907–1973)*

Is this the party to whom I am speaking?

Lily Tomlin as Ernestine the operator

Let others praise ancient times; I am glad I was born in
these. *Ovid (43 B.C.–A.D. 18)*

542

Happiness is good health and a bad memory.
Ingrid Bergman (1917–1982)

543

Never keep up with the Joneses. Drag them down to your level.   *Quentin Crisp*

544

People who think they know everything are very irritating to those of us who do.   *Unknown*

545

I want a house that has got over all its troubles; I don't want to spend the rest of my life bringing up a young and inexperienced house.
Jerome K. Jerome (1859–1927)

546

There is something about a closet that makes a skeleton restless.   *Unknown*

547

By dint of railing at idiots you run the risk of becoming idiotic yourself.

Gustave Flaubert (1821–1880)

548

There is no gravity. The earth sucks.   *Graffito*

549

When the going gets tough, the smart get lost.

Robert Byrne

550

Miss Erickson looked more peculiar than ever this morning. Is her spiritualism getting worse?

Noel Coward (1889–1973)

551

I shot an arrow into the air, and it stuck.

Graffito in Los Angeles

552

There's so much pollution in the air now that if it weren't for our lungs there'd be no place to put it all.

Robert Orben

553

I don't know how old I am because the goat ate the Bible that had my birth certificate in it. The goat lived to be twenty-seven.

Satchel Paige (1906?-1982)

554

Nothing ever goes away.   *Barry Commoner*

555

There's nothing wrong with you that reincarnation won't cure.

Jack E. Leonard (1911-1973) to
Ed Sullivan (1902-1974)

556

A lie is an abomination unto the Lord and a very present help in time of trouble.

Adlai Stevenson (1900-1965)

557

During a carnival men put masks over their masks.
Xavier Forneret, 1838

558

One hundred thousand lemmings can't be wrong.
Graffito

559

He was the world's only armless sculptor. He put the chisel in his mouth and his wife hit him on the back of the head with a mallet. *Fred Allen (1894–1956)*

560

Modern art is what happens when painters stop looking at girls and persuade themselves that they have a better idea. *John Ciardi*

561

Either this wallpaper goes or I do.
*Almost certainly not the last words of
Oscar Wilde (1856–1900)*

562

A life spent making mistakes is not only more honorable but more useful than a life spent doing nothing.
George Bernard Shaw (1856–1950)

563

Friends may come and go, but enemies accumulate.
Thomas Jones

564

When down in the mouth, remember Jonah. He came out all right. *Thomas Edison (1847–1931)*

565

Retirement at sixty-five is ridiculous. When I was sixty-five I still had pimples. *George Burns*

566

Old age is the only disease you don't look forward to being cured of. *From the movie* Citizen Kane, *1941*

567

Start every day off with a smile and get it over with.
W. C. Fields (1880–1946)

568

I took a course in speed reading and was able to read *War and Peace* in twenty minutes. It's about Russia.
Woody Allen

569

When your IQ rises to 28, sell.
Professor Irwin Corey to a heckler

570

Some people are like popular songs that you only sing for a short time.   *La Rochefoucauld (1613–1680)*

571

George the Third
Ought never to have occurred.
One can only wonder
At so grotesque a blunder.
Edmund Clerihew (1875–1956)

There are two kinds of pedestrians . . . the quick and the dead.

Lord Thomas Robert Dewar (1864–1930)

I used to work in a fire hydrant factory. You couldn't park anywhere near the place.   *Steven Wright*

I don't have any trouble parking. I drive a forklift.

Jim Samuels

God help those who do not help themselves.

Wilson Mizner (1876–1933)

There is only one good substitute for the endearments of a sister, and that is the endearments of some other fellow's sister.   *Josh Billings (1818–1885)*

577

When smashing monuments, save the pedestals—they
always come in handy. *Stanislaw Lem*

578

Great men are not always idiots.
Karen Elizabeth Gordon

579

Few great men could pass Personnel.
Paul Goodman (1911–1972)

580

Fanaticism consists of redoubling your effort when you have forgotten your aim.
George Santayana (1863–1952)

581

Mountains appear more lofty the nearer they are approached, but great men resemble them not in this particular.
Lady Marguerite Blessington (1789–1849)

582

There's a great woman behind every idiot.
John Lennon (1941–1980) on Yoko Ono

583

Nothing is more conducive to peace of mind than not having any opinions at all.
Georg Christoph Lichtenberg (1742–1799)

584

The mome rath isn't born that could outgrabe me.
Nicol Williamson

585

If you live to the age of a hundred you have it made because very few people die past the age of a hundred.
George Burns

586

Never accept an invitation from a stranger unless he gives you candy. *Linda Festa*

587

You can choose your friends, but you only have one mother. *Max Shulman*

One is not superior merely because one sees the world as odious. *Chateaubriand (1768–1848)*

If it weren't for the last minute, nothing would get done. *Unknown*

If I were a grave-digger or even a hangman, there are some people I could work for with a great deal of enjoyment. *Douglas Jerrold (1803–1857)*

It is easier to forgive an enemy than to forgive a friend. *William Blake (1757–1827)*

592

You are no bigger than the things that annoy you.
Jerry Bundsen

593

It is unpleasant to go alone, even to be drowned.
Russian proverb

594

Stay with me; I want to be alone.   *Joey Adams*

595

They made love only during total eclipses of the sun because they wouldn't take off their clothes unless it was dark in the entire world. *Unknown*

596

We are what we pretend to be. *Kurt Vonnegut, Jr.*

597

Thank you, but I have other plans.
Response to "Have a nice day"
suggested by Paul Fussell

598

WARNING TO ALL PERSONNEL
Firings will continue until moral improves.
Unknown

599

Do we really deserve top billing?
Fred Allen (1894–1956) to Henry Morgan at a
meeting of the National Conference of
Christians and Jews

600

Psychics will lead dogs to your body.
Alleged fortune cookie message

601

I don't worry about crime in the streets; it's the sidewalks I stay off of.   *Johnson Letellier*

602

Carney's Law: There's at least a 50-50 chance that someone will print the name Craney incorrectly.
Jim Canrey

603

Bad spellers of the world, untie!   *Graffito*

604

Complete this sentence:
I never met a man I didn't like
   a. to cheat.
   b. at first.
   c. to avoid.
   d. better than you.   *Robert Byrne*

Fix this sentence:

He put the horse before the cart.   *Stephen Price*

I am firm. You are obstinate. He is a pig-headed fool.
Katharine Whitehorn

Dr. Livingstone I Presume
Full name of Dr. Presume

Unknown

A language is a dialect with an army and navy.
Max Weinreich (1894–1969)

I can't seem to bring myself to say, "Well, I guess I'll be toddling along." It isn't that I can't toddle. It's that I can't guess I'll toddle.

Robert Benchley (1889–1945)

610

Hamlet as performed at the Brooklyn Shakespeare Festival:

"To be, or what?"

Steven Pearl

611

Smoking is, as far as I'm concerned, the entire point of being an adult.   *Fran Lebowitz*

612

A steam engine has always got character. It's the most human of all man-made machines.

Reverend William Vere Awdrey

613

There is only one word for aid that is genuinely without strings, and that word is blackmail.

Colm Brogan

614

Al didn't smile for forty years. You've got to admire a man like that.

From the television series
"Mary Hartman, Mary Hartman"

615

All professions are conspiracies against the laity.
George Bernard Shaw (1856–1950)

616

Very few people do anything creative after the age of thirty-five. The reason is that very few people do anything creative before the age of thirty-five.
Joel Hildebrand (1881–1983)

617

There is no they, only us. *Bumper sticker*

618

I was in a beauty contest once. I not only came in last,
I was hit in the mouth by Miss Congeniality.

Phyllis Diller

619

You can get more with a kind word and a gun than you
can with a kind word alone.   *Johnny Carson*

620

I think it would be a good idea.

*Mahatma Gandhi (1869–1948) when asked
what he thought of Western civilization*

621

Remember that a kick in the ass is a step forward.

Unknown

622

What is algebra, exactly? Is it those three-cornered
things? *J. M. Barrie (1860–1937)*

623

Computers are useless. They can only give you answers.
Pablo Picasso (1881–1973)

624

Peace, n. In international affairs, a period of cheating between two periods of fighting.
Ambrose Bierce (1842–1914?)

625

Let thy maid servant be faithful, strong, and homely.
Benjamin Franklin (1706–1790)

626

At twenty-six, Kate, though not promiscuous, had slept with most of the decent men in public life.
Renata Adler

627

The egg cream is psychologically the opposite of circumcision—it *pleasurably* reaffirms your Jewishness.
Mel Brooks

628

His absence is good company. *Scottish saying*

629

The happiest liaisons are based on mutual misunderstanding. *La Rochefoucauld (1613–1680)*

So many beautiful women and so little time.

John Barrymore (1882–1942)

The art of *not* reading is extremely important. It consists in our not taking up whatever happens to occupy the larger public.   *Arthur Schopenhauer (1788–1860)*

Nowadays the illiterates can read and write.

Alberto Moravia

A good man is always a beginner.

Martial (c. 40–c. 104)

I knew a very interesting Italian woman last winter, but now she's married.

Percy Bysshe Shelley (1792–1822)

635

How much money did you make last year? Mail it in.
Simplified tax form
suggested by Stanton Delaplane

636

Gray hair is God's graffiti.   *Bill Cosby*

637

The gods too are fond of a joke.
Aristotle (384–322 B.C.*)*

Sources, References, and Notes

cᴀ⊕ᴴ⊚ᴈ

Like other books of quotations, this one owes a heavy debt to anthologists who have gone before. The principal secondary sources I used in supplementing my own reading and eavesdropping are listed below and referred to in the citations by the letters assigned to them.

Readers who point out misquotations or supply missing sources will be thanked in future printings, if any. Favorite lines (nothing pompous, please) also will be gratefully received.

Collecting quotations is an insidious, even embarrassing habit, like ragpicking or hoarding rocks or trying on other people's laundry. I got into it originally while trying to break an addiction to candy. I kicked candy and now seem to be stuck with quotations, which are attacking my brain instead of my teeth. While I have no plans to compile a third sampler, I can't promise I won't, either.

A. H. L. Mencken, ed., *A New Dictionary of Quotations on Historical Principles* (New York: Alfred A. Knopf, 1952).

B. Jonathon Green, comp., *Morrow's International Dictionary of Contemporary Quotations* (New York: William Morrow and Company, 1982).

C. J. M. and M. J. Cohen, *The Penguin Dictionary of Modern Quotations*, 2nd ed. (Harmondsworth, England, and New York: Penguin Books, 1980).

D. John Gross, comp., *The Oxford Book of Aphorisms* (Oxford, England: Oxford University Press, 1983.)

E. Gerald F. Lieberman, *3,500 Good Quotes for Speakers* (New York: Doubleday & Company, 1983).

F. Bob Chieger, *Was It Good for You, Too? Quotations on Love and Sex* (New York: Atheneum Publishers, 1983).

G. Jonathon Green, comp., *The Book of Political Quotes* (New York: McGraw-Hill Book Company, 1982).

H. Joe Franklin, *Joe Franklin's Encyclopedia of Comedians* (Secaucus, N.J.: Citadel Press, 1979).

I. Steve Allen, *More Funny People* (New York: Stein and Day, 1982).

2. As given in D.
3. *Notebooks*, 1912.
4. As given in C.
5. Quoted in the *New York Times Book Review*, October 30, 1933.
8. Linda Festa to RB.
9. As given in *Peter's Quotations* (New York: William Morrow and Company, 1977).
10. "The Tonight Show," September 31, 1982.
12. As given in D.
14. "The Tonight Show," August 11, 1982.
15. Thanks to Ms. Christopher B. Eubanks.
16. As given in E.
18. Thanks to Robert Machuta.
19. As given in F.
20. As given in D.
22. From *The Ladies Guide* (Battle Creek, Mich.: Modern Medicine Publishing Company, 1895). Dr. Kellogg helped invent cornflakes and peanut butter. In addition to denouncing masturbation, he believed that smoking caused cancer and that certain ailments could be cured by rolling a cannonball on the stomach.
23. As quoted by John Molloy in a San Francisco lecture in 1982.
24. A slightly different version is in E.
27. From the movie *Sleeper*.
28. As given in *Quotations for Writers and Speakers*, by A. Andrews.
29. As given in B.
32. Thanks to George Dushek.
35. As given in *Wihelm Meisters Lehrjahre*, 1795.
37. As given in A.
38. Linda Festa to RB.
39. Quoted in the *San Francisco Chronicle*, August 14, 1982.
40. As given in Walter Wagner, *You Must Remember This*.
41. As given in F.
42. At Cobb's Pub, San Francisco, February 3, 1984.
43. During the San Francisco Standup Comedy Competition, 1983.
44. From the movie *Everything You Wanted to Know About Sex*.
45. As given in *The Sayings of Quentin Crisp*.
47. As given in B.
48. As given in Charlotte Chandler, *The Ultimate Seduction*.
49. As given in Joseph Weintraub, ed., *The Wit and Wisdom of Mae West*.
50. As given in E.
51, 52. As given in C.
57. Thanks to Arlene Heath.
59. As given in *Who Do You Think You Are*?

61. As given in *The Well-Tempered Sentence* (New York: Ticknor & Fields).
65. As given in H.
68. As given in F.
71. Don Rose is a San Francisco disk jockey.
72. Thanks to Arlene Heath.
73. Martin Cruz Smith to RB in jest.
76. As given in E.
78. As given in B.
79. Jim Samuels won the 1982 San Francisco Standup Comedy Competition.
80. *Newsweek*, 1980
82. As given in B.
84. As given in *Comment*.
85. As given in F.
92. As quoted by Merla Zellerbach in the *San Francisco Chronicle*, December 21, 1982.
93. Thanks to Charles DeShong.
94. As given in *The Young Duke*, 1831.
96. Interview in the *Washington Post*, January 1983.
99, 100. As given in F.
101. From the movie *Manhattan*.
103. As given in *The Watched Pot*.
106. As given in *One Fat Englishman*.
107. As given in H.
109, 110. As given in A.
111. As given in Newbern and Rodebaugh, *Proverbs of the World*.
112. As given in *Vital Parts*. Thanks to Gerald Howard.
113, 114. As given in E.
115. As given in *The British Museum Is Falling Down*.
116. As given in *The Lonely Life*.
118. Robert Orben is a professional joke writer who publishes a newsletter called *Orben's Current Comedy* that is airmailed to subscribers. This is from the November 2, 1983, edition. The address is 700 Orange Street, Wilmington, Delaware 19801.
119. As given in E.
120. As given in *Last Words*, 1933.
123. As given in *The Measure of My Days*, 1972.
125. As given in *Newsweek*, 1978.
126. As given in B.
128. As given in Frank Muir, *The Frank Muir Book*.
129. As given in *The Old Woman*.
130. As recalled by Arlene Heath.
131. As given in *Time*, December 28, 1970.
133. As given in *Living It Up*.
134. As given in *Reginald in Russia*, 1910.
135. From the movie *Annie Hall*.
138. Thanks to Cyra McFadden.

139. Quoted by Georgia Hesse in the *San Francisco Chronicle*. Hesse added that Dom Pérignon was blind at the time.

144. As given in Herb Caen's *San Francisco Chronicle* column, November 24, 1983.

145. As given in B.

147, 148. As given in H.

149. As given in Gary Herman, comp., *The Book of Hollywood Quotes* (London: Omnibus Press, 1979). Thanks to Chris Arnold.

150. Quoted by Jimmy Breslin in his syndicated column, April 1983.

151. As given in B.

153. From *Rhinoceros*, Act II.

154. Bill Musselman is a basketball coach.

157. From the movie *Sleeper*.

160. As given in the *Observer*, April 19, 1957.

161. From *Death of a Salesman*.

162. From Larry Gelbart's introduction to I.

163. As given in *Funny, but Not Vulgar*, 1944.

164, 165. From Mordecai Richler's introduction to *The Best of Modern Humor* (New York: Alfred A. Knopf, 1983).

167. As given in Calvin Trillin's San Francisco lecture, January 18, 1984.

168. From a cable TV special called "Homage to Steve," 1984.

171. As given in *Sisterhood Is Powerful*.

174. As given in B.

175. As given in E.

176. As given in *Metropolitan Life*.

177. As given in E.

178. As given in *Kiss and Tell*.

179. As given in *Quote and Unquote*.

180. As given in B.

184. As given in *Esquire*, 1970.

184. See note 151.

189. See note 92.

190. As given in *The Saturday Evening Post*, 1952

191. A slightly different version is given in F.

193. As given in *MS* (November 1983).

194. As given in the movie *The Culture of Narcissism* (1979).

195. As given in *I'm No Angel*.

196. From Gerald Nachman's column in the *San Francisco Chronicle*, August 1982.

197. As given in B.

201. As given in *The Big Book of Jewish Humor*.

202. From the movie *My Favorite Year*.

203. As given by S. M. Ulam, *Adventures of a Mathematician* (New York: Charles Scribner's Sons, 1976).

207. As given in *The Conquest of Happiness*.

210. As given in B.

218. As given in *Jackie Mason's America* (Lyle Stuart, Inc., 1983).
219. As given in *The Painted Lady*.
220. Thanks to Linda Festa.
222. As given in *Careers for Women*.
227. See note 92.
232. Quoted by Herb Caen in the *San Francisco Chronicle*, May 17, 1983.
233. *New Yorker*, January 2, 1984.
234. As given in E.
235. As given in the *Village Voice*, April 1983.
238. As given in G.
240. As given in Joseph Heller, *Catch-22*.
242. As given in E.
243. As given in G.
244. From Will Rogers, *Autobiography*.
247. From *The Tonight Show*, February 8, 1984.
248. At The Punch Line, San Francisco, January 1984.
249. Herb Caen's column, *San Francisco Chronicle*, August 19, 1983.
251. From an article in *The San Francisco Paper*, February 1984.
252. As given in D.
253. As given in J. Green, *The Book of Rock Quotes*.
257. As given in A.
259. See note 218.
265. See note 218.
267. As given in *Orben's Current Comedy*, October 19, 1983.
268. See note 92.
272. Recalled by Calvin Trillin.
274. Thanks to Arlene Heath.
275. As given in B.
276. As given in H.
278. As given in *The Daily Herald*, October 5, 1962.
279. Quoted by Paul Burka in *Esquire* (April 1983).
280. As given in Andy Rooney, *And More by Andy Rooney*.
281. See note 92.
283. *The Tonight Show*, September 26, 1983.
284. Gerald Nachman is a columnist for the *San Francisco Chronicle*.
285. As given in *The Hole*.
286. Quoted by Sir Laurence Olivier on the BBC.
290. See note 92.
292, 293. See note 167.
294. As given in B.
296. As given in Herb Caen's column, *San Francisco Chronicle*, December 2, 1982.
297. As given in *The Letters of Edna St. Vincent Millay*.
298. As given in *The Men's Club*.
299. Quoted by Richard Condon in *Prizzi's Honor*.
303. Quoted by Paul Fussell in *Class*.

304. See note 92.
305. As given in D.
306. As given in the *Observer*, April 20, 1958.
307. As given in C.
310. As given in G.
311. *The Third Man* was written by Graham Greene.
313. From the TV show "Late Night with David Letterman," January 6, 1984.
314. From his nightly commentary on Channel 4 (NBC), San Francisco, September 28, 1982.
315. From her San Francisco lecture, November 4, 1983.
316. From "Late Night with David Letterman," February 9, 1984.
317. From a letter to Goodman Ace.
320. Will Durst won the 1983 San Francisco Standup Comedy Competition.
322. See note 248.
324. "The Tonight Show," September 14, 1983.
327. As given in H.
328. As given in D.
333. As given in E.
337. As given in D.
342. Thanks to Tom Stewart.
349. As given in *The Critic as Artist*, 1891.
350. Written for a competition among the paper's sub-editors for "the world's most boring headline." Described by Claud Cockburn in his *Autobiography*.
351. Cecilia Bartholomew writes and teaches writing in the San Francisco area.
352. Quoted by George Will in his syndicated column, December 20, 1983.
353. In the *New York Times Book Review*, January 1, 1984.
355. As given in B.
360. As given in *The Nature and Aim of Fiction*. Thanks to Gerald Howard.
363. As given in the *New York Times Book Review*, June 6, 1982.
364. *Afterthoughts*, 1931.
365. As given in the *Observer*, October 14, 1951.
367. As given in the *Guardian*, March 21, 1973.
369. As given in F. Scott Fitzgerald, *The Last Tycoon*.
371. As given in the *Sunday Times* (London), October 16, 1977.
372. As given in *Time*, 1957.
373. Quoted by W. H. Auden in *A Certain World*.
378, 379, 380. See note 151.
381. As given in the *New York Times Book Review*, 1971.
382. As given in the *Observer*, October 8, 1961.
383. As given in H.
398. From the movie *All About Eve*, 1950.
400. As given in *San Francisco Chronicle*, December 21, 1982.

401. As given in *San Francisco Chronicle*, January 2, 1983.
402. Arthur Gingold wrote *Items from Our Catalog*.
403. Quoted by Gerald Nachman in the *San Francisco Chronicle*, September 22, 1983.
404. Quoted by Gerald Nachman in the *San Francisco Chronicle*, July 18, 1983.
405. Quoted by Gerald Nachman in the *San Francisco Chronicle*, December 21, 1983.
407. As given in the *New York Times Magazine*, January 9, 1966.
408. As given in B.
412. As given in E.
413. Martin Cruz Smith to RB.
415. As given in F.
416. As given in C.
419. Thanks to Maureen Connolly.
427. See note 79.
429. From a Hallmark card.
435. As given in *A Madman's Diary*.
436. As given in *More in Anger*, 1958.
437. Inge was dean of St. Paul's.
438. See note 79.
439. From the radio show *The Prairie Home Companion*, June 1983.
442 As given in *Cat Scan* (New York: Atheneum, 1983.
444. Thanks to Leslie Sheridan.
446. As given in *The Diary of Alice James*.
448. As given in I.
449. As given in E.
450. As given in *Jeeves and the Hard-boiled Egg*.
452. Quoted by Harry Zohn, *Karl Kraus*.
453. As given in the *Observer*, July 19, 1975.
455. "The Tonight Show," February 10, 1984.
456. As given in the *Atlantic Monthly*, 1981.
459. As given in A. Schlesinger, Jr., *A Thousand Days*.
460, 461. As given in G.
462. As given in H.
464. As given in B.
467. "The Tonight Show," November 17, 1982.
470. See note 315.
479. Thanks to Charles T. DeShong.
485. As given in *The Book of Laughter and Forgetting*.
487. Thanks to Dick Werthimer.
488. Thanks to Robert Machuta.
490. Thanks to Charles T. DeShong.
491. Darrin Weinberg to RB.
493. See note 248.
495. John Rostoni to Teressa Skelton to RB.
499. Often called Sturgeon's Law.
500. *Improvisation*.

503. See note 61.
504. As given in *The Naked Civil Servant*.
507. As given in D.
508. As given in *Psychology in the Wry*.
514. Don Quisenberry is a baseball pitcher.
517. Teressa Skelton to RB.
518. Thanks to Bob Hudson.
520. See note 92.
521. Quoted by Herb Caen in the *San Francisco Chronicle*, May 22, 1983.
523. As given in *Orben's Current Comedy*, September 21, 1983. See note 118.
525. As given in I.
526. As given in *My Saber Is Bent*, 1983. See note 118.
530. As given in *The Bald Twit Lion*.
532. As given in *Epistles*.
543. As given in *How to Become a Virgin*.
545. As given in *They and I*.
550. As given in *Present Laughter*, Act I.
552. As given in *Orben's Current Comedy*, November 17, 1983. See note 118.
556. As given in G.
557. See slightly different wording in D.
558. As given in C.
559. As given in I.
563. As given in the *Wall Street Journal*, 1975.
565. See note 151.
570. *Maxims*, 1665.
572. As given in George Robey, *Looking Back on Life*.
573. "The Tonight Show," September 14, 1983.
577. As given in *Unkempt Thoughts*.
581. As given in *Night Thought Book*, 1834.
586. Linda Festa to RB.
590. As given in *Ugly Trades*.
592. Jerry Bundsen is a former aide to Herb Caen, who quoted this line in his column in the *San Francisco Chronicle* in October 1983.
594. As given in H.
596. In the introduction to *Mother Night*.
597. As given in *Class*.
599. As given in I.
602. Quoted in the magazine *Friendly Exchange* (Winter 1982).
605. As given in *The Densa Quiz*.
606. As given in the *Observer*, 1974.
607. Thanks to Arlene Heath.
609. See note 151.
611. As given in *Social Studies*.
612, 613. As given in B.

615. Thanks to George Dushek.
618. As given in F.
622. As given in *Quality Street*, Act III.
623. As given in William Fifield, *In Search of Genius*.
624. As given in *The Devil's Dictionary*.
625. As given in *Poor Richard's Almanac*.
626. As given in *Speedboat*. Thanks to Gerald Howard.
629. Thanks to George Dushek.
631. As given in *On Reading and Books*, 1851.
634. As given in letter to T. J. Hogg, 1821.
635. As given in Stanton Delaplane's column in the *San Francisco Chronicle*, March 7, 1934.
636. "The Tonight Show," March 13, 1984.

Index of Authors

Index of Subjects and Key Words

The author at the start of his
quest for the world's best quotes

*Robert Byrne's love of the succinct has driven him to
compile three anthologies:* The 637 Best Things Anybody
Ever Said, Cat Scan—All the Best from the Literature of
Cats, *with Teressa Skelton, and this present volume. His
twelve published books suggest, however, that he is more
than a mere collector of other people's pith. He can write
things himself.*

The author today